HOW TO WRITE A SERIES

A Guide to Series Types and Structure plus Troubleshooting Tips and Marketing Tactics

SARA ROSETT

McGuffin Ink

HOW TO WRITE A SERIES

A Guide to Series Types and Structure plus Troubleshooting Tips and Marketing Tactics

Book Two in the Genre Fiction How To series

Published by McGuffin Ink

Textbook ISBN: 978-1-950054-33-6

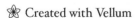 Created with Vellum

To my IRL writer friends,
Jami and Danielle, who have been there with me as I completed
two series and began another.
Here's to many more for all of us!

INTRODUCTION

> "*Write what you know.*"
> —*often attributed to Mark Twain*

Write a series is a piece of advice that new writers hear over and over again. It's an often-quoted mantra like *read in your genre* and *write what you know*. Veteran authors point to these basic premises as keys to success in publishing.

Read in your genre and *write what you know* are pretty self-explanatory, and at first glance the advice to write a series might seem to be self-explanatory (write books linked through a protagonist or another element like a setting).

But I discovered writing a series is a deep and complex topic, yet there's little guidance for authors on how to put individual books together in a way that's satisfying for readers. Most writing advice focuses on how to produce a single book. Few writing craft resources discuss the nuts and bolts of series writing.

MY EXPERIENCE

When I sat down to write my first book I felt pretty confident about a few things. I was a cozy reader. *Know your genre:* check! My protagonist was a military spouse. I was a military spouse. *Write what you know:* check! My confidence faltered a bit at the advice to write a series.

I had no idea what I was doing when it came to writing a series, and I only found a few blog posts on the topic. But I knew the book I was writing would be Book One of a series because it was a cozy mystery. A stand-alone cozy is rare, practically non-existent!

I decided to focus on the task at hand and get Book One written. I worked my way through a multitude of drafts and revisions until I had a book. The concept of that book as part of a series remained a shadowy idea, barely on my radar.

WHAT'S NEXT?

When I finished editing and revising my first mystery I had rough concepts for the next few books. I had ideas for the mysteries in the next few books, but the only plan I had for the series element was that the main character, who was a military spouse, would move every few books, which would help the series avoid "Cabot Cove" syndrome.

If you're familiar with *Murder, She Wrote*, you know that the small town where Jessica Fletcher lived, Cabot Cove, was plagued by an unusually high murder rate, a situation that strains believability after a few murderous incidents. I figured with my protagonist's built-in ability to move around, I'd solved one problem with writing a series.

I didn't think about other elements of the series, or how the protagonist and her situation would impact the books over the long term. I didn't consider the limitations I'd face with a mom of a baby as a sleuth. She had to be responsible and find child care every time she went sleuthing, which became one of the most annoying parts of plotting each book. I didn't think about how giving the series a "reset" by moving it to a new location every few books could cause problems if readers were following the journeys of supporting characters. (They'd have to move too!)

And speaking of supporting characters, I also didn't

think twice about the ages of the kids in the series—about how fast or slow they'd age or about how their growing up would impact the series. The antics and activities of the kids provided some of the humor and also gave readers whose kids were grown the ability to indulge in nostalgia. As they read about Ellie's kids, they enjoyed remembering when their kids were young. If the kids in the series grew up, would readers still be interested in Ellie without her band of cute Pre-K kids tagging along?

ITERATION . . . AND MORE ITERATION

The issues I encountered while writing the Ellie books lead me to formulate a completely different type of character for my second series and to have a more thought-out plan for the On the Run series. That plan turned out to be a little too strict and had to be modified. I went from one end of the spectrum (very little planning) to the other (a plan that was too limiting). I learned how to expand a series beyond my original vision of a trilogy.

With my next two series, I feel I've hit a happy medium of creating a flexible plan that I can modify if I need to. I've learned how to think ahead and envision issues that could be problems. I've learned how to keep track of details. I've created a spin-off series and created a literary universe that can sustain several different series. I've also had to decide it was time to end a series.

Everything I've learned about writing a series has been through trial and error. I hope my lessons-learned will give you a shortcut when it comes to writing your series, help you avoid writing yourself into a corner, and spark ideas for your series.

A NOTE ON THE EXAMPLES IN THIS BOOK

I've tried to include a variety of examples throughout the book from many different genres. To make the examples as accessible as possible, I've tried to stick with series that are well-known.

Please don't be upset if I didn't include your favorite series. There are so many wonderful series that I wasn't able to include all my favorites either! I also included examples from my own series. I've made plenty of mistakes and hope sharing my lessons help you make smart choices for your series.

Because this is a book about writing *book* series, I've avoided using movie and television series as examples. Many of the book series mentioned have been adapted to the small or big screen (sometimes both) but examples always refer to the original book series.

This is a high-level overview of how to write a series, which focuses on how the elements of fiction (character arcs, subplots, setting, etc.) function in a series. There are many wonderful books dedicated to these individual elements.

If you want a deep dive on one of the separate elements, say how to write great character arcs or world-building, then dig into a book or course on that specific topic. For this book, we'll concentrate on the big picture of how the elements of fiction work together to create a compelling series.

QUESTIONS:

Make a list of your favorite series books. Do you see any similarities?

Do they have the same type of protagonist?

_____

_____

_____

_____

_____

_____

_____

Are there any common themes or subplots?

_____

_____

_____

_____

_____

_____

_____

If you've written a series before, list what was successful about it.

_____

_____

_____

_____

_____

_____

_____

Also take a moment to list the problems you encountered.

_____

_____

_____

_____

_____

_____

_____

WHY WRITE A SERIES?

> 66 *"The problem with books is that they end."*
> *—Caroline Kepnes*

Let's start at the beginning: why writing a series is a good idea. Then we'll look at some of the challenges involved with writing a series as well as some of the drawbacks.

READERS LOVE A SERIES

The first reason to write a series is straightforward—readers love them! Once you've written Book One in a series readers know what to expect and you can fulfill that expectation again and again. Returning to the world and characters you've created is like spending time with old friends. And yet it's a new story, so you've fulfilled that classic Hollywood request that Blake Snyder describes in *Save The Cat*.

> "*Give me the same thing . . . only different.*"
> —*Blake Snyder*

Readers know the promises you made them and look forward to returning to that same type of "read." If you wrote a dark gritty mystery, then they'll expect more books with a similar tone and style. You can fulfill the expectation again and again. Meeting readers' expectations means that they're happy and will continue to look for your books.

FINANCIAL STABILITY

If you have happy readers who return again and again, you'll have a good income stream. Writing a series is a great way to stabilize your income. Once you have several books out, you can make the reasonable assumption that another book in a series will perform at a certain level.

A SERIES CAN BE MORE TIME-EFFICIENT

With standalone books, you create new worlds, characters, and themes with each book, but with a series you return to familiar territory.

Your protagonist and possibly your location as well as several secondary characters are already established, which means it may take you less time to write the book. It may not. Each book is its own beast and some of them just take longer to write than others, but with a series you at least have a familiar starting point.

ABILITY TO GO DEEPER AND EXPLORE MORE COMPLEX THEMES

Perhaps you have a complex storyline or theme. With a series you can take your time and fully explore the intricacies of the themes and subplots over the course of several books.

Many authors find writing a series creatively satisfying. They like the openness a series allows, which gives them the freedom to experiment and fully explore their ideas.

THE CHALLENGES AND DRAWBACKS

The Dichotomy of Writing a Series

Writing a series is a challenging dichotomy. You want to create satisfying and complete novels, yet the novels contain threads to pull the reader from book to book. It's a balancing act. You want your readers to have a good reading experience in each book, and you want to fulfill reader expectations in each book.

If you're writing romance, you definitely want a "happily ever after" or a "happy for now" ending. Mystery readers expect to find out "whodunit." Thriller readers will be upset if you don't have a final confrontation with the big baddie who's been tormenting the protagonist throughout the book. So how do you make each book satisfying and at the same time make the individual novels part of a larger series?

You meet genre expectations in each book, but each book contains a bigger story, an over-arching story, theme, or trope that connects the books. The threads of that overarching story pull the reader from book to book. The couple in the romance are part of a bigger community, like a family or a set of friends.

The reader saw Tom and Chloe fall in love, but what about Tom's feisty sister or Chloe's geeky best friend? Will those characters find their happily ever after?

And the sleuth who solved the mystery, what will happen to her? Will her annoying ex-husband, who caused her nothing but trouble in the first book, pull her into another mystery . . . perhaps by turning up as a dead body in Book Two? What if the protagonist in the thriller defeats the big baddie, but then realizes there's an even bigger bad guy?

. . .

Drawbacks

While writing a series lets you play with a larger canvas than a single book allows, there are drawbacks as well. We'll take a quick look at the downsides of writing a series here, then in the Ending a Series chapter and the Troubleshooting chapter we'll look at ways to deal with these problems.

- ### *Boredom*

Series characters and situations can go stale both for the author and the reader. First, let's look at the situation when an author becomes bored with a series. Agatha Christie wanted to kill off Poirot, according to her grandson, who stated in an interview with the *Radio Times* that she was "very keen to exorcise herself of him by writing different stories with new characters."[1]

Sir Arthur Conan Doyle did kill off Sherlock Holmes, but fans were outraged, and 20,000 canceled their subscription to the *Strand* magazine according to a *BBC* article.[2] Eventually Doyle resurrected Holmes. In a best-case scenario, your creation—whether it's a series character or a series world—may take off, and you could be writing it for a long time, which is all the more reason to think carefully about the construction of your series.

- ### *Immutability*

Once you've begun publishing books in your series, you're locked in. Did you make your sleuth too young or too old? Did you create a world that has too many limits and makes it hard to continue the series? Those are big-picture problems, but you also have the same issue with smaller details.

Does your protagonist drive a Honda Accord in Book One? If you randomly change her car to a BMW in Book Two fans will wonder what happened to the Accord. It's a small continuity issue that may not seem important, but when you have hundreds of small details recorded in the first books in your series, you have to keep up with them. If you don't, your true fans will be disappointed, if not upset.

• *Success Depends on the Quality of the First Book*

In Episode 216 of the Novel Marketing podcast, Thomas Umstattd, Jr. pointed out that if you're writing a series, the success of it hinges on the first book. If your Book One is poorly written, then readers probably won't go on to read the rest of the series.

It's a catch-22 for authors because as we write more, our books get better, but readers usually want to start with the first book in a series. Your Book Five may be the best book you've ever written, but because it's later in the series many readers won't give it a try if they didn't enjoy the first book.

• *Ending a Series*

Ending a series can be problematic. Readers get attached to series characters. They don't want the story to end. This situation can lead to several problems. The first occurs when an author keeps writing a series long after it should have ended. The writer may continue producing books in the series because the readers who are super fans want more books in the series.

Or the author keeps writing in the same series because they know a book in that series will bring a certain amount of income. The stories become retreads. The author finds writing the series onerous and terms like "phoning it in" begin to appear in reviews. Another problem with ending a series is that readers may not move on to the author's next project. They're so attached to the series they love that they don't want to read anything else from the author.

Remember there are ways around each of these problems, and we'll explore them in more depth in the Ending a Series and Troubleshooting chapters.

TYPES OF SERIES

If we look at the big picture, series generally fall into one of two broad groups. They're either a multi-protagonist series or a single protagonist series.

The single protagonist series can be broken down further into sub-categories, but for now let's just look at the multi-protagonist series. First, we'll examine each element of the series, then look at some specific examples.

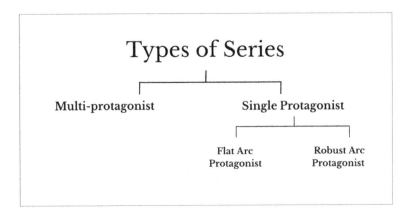

MULTI-PROTAGONIST SERIES

In a multi-protagonist series each book has a new protagonist, but those protagonists are linked in some way. Each book is self-contained, and the books can be read in any order. This type of structure is found most frequently in romance.

ANTAGONIST

A multi-protagonist series may have an antagonist or not. In romantic suspense, there is often an identifiable antagonist, but in contemporary romance, there's usually not a villain trying to keep the two characters apart. The antagonistic forces are within each of the characters. The character's own beliefs and world views create roadblocks to the Happily Ever After.

SETTING

The setting is often the element that links the books together, but that's not required. If the setting does connect the books, it might be a small town, a business, or a neighborhood.

Make sure the setting appeals to fans of your genre, and world-build accordingly. Fans of small-town romance probably won't be as interested in a book set in Manhattan, but readers who enjoy billionaire romance would snap up that book.

SECONDARY CHARACTERS

Secondary characters often become the main characters in subsequent books. Two secondary characters in one book may become one of the protagonists in another book.

This shifting of the spotlight from one character (or from one couple) to another has several benefits. It keeps the series fresh. It allows the author to deepen the relationships between the characters, and it lets the readers revisit favorite characters later in time and get a glimpse of how they've changed, such as after the wedding or after they've had a baby.

SUBPLOTS

Instead of having a single entry point at Book One, a reader can pick up any book in a multi-protagonist series and begin reading there. Because the multi-protagonist series is structured in an episodic way, you may not have extremely complex subplots that flow through the series, which create a need to read books in a certain order for the overarching story to make sense.

However, there are some multi-protagonist series, such as the Black Dagger Brotherhood by J.R. Ward, that do have an overarching subplot that carries through the series.

Subplots in multi-protagonist series often revolve around the secondary characters, who will later become the main characters in future books, or around the unifying element of the series, such as a setting or trope.

LENGTH

Depending on the structure of the series, this type of series can be limitless. You can keep expanding the universe of the series, adding more and more books as long as you didn't limit yourself in the beginning.

If your original premise was a series about three sisters who each find romance, then it will be a bit more of a challenge to expand beyond those sisters, but it can be done. Someone could discover a long-lost sibling, right? Or perhaps you pivot and explore the lives of the parents or a cousin's story.

Since this type of series structure is often used in romance, let's look at a few examples from that genre and the linking devices used to create series cohesion.

EXAMPLES FROM THE ROMANCE GENRE

Family

Probably the most common way to link multi-protagonist series is through family relationships. Bella Andre's Sullivan series explores how the members of an extended family find love. Mary Balogh uses the same structure in historical romance.

Friend or Group

The link can be through a friendship group, like a group of girls who have been best friends since they were kids or a set of women who participate in a book club. All the protagonists might work at the same office. In Nora Robert's Bride Quartet series, the protagonists work at a wedding planning company.

Another way to link books is through a group or association. J.R. Ward's Black Dagger Brotherhood is a series of novels about a society of vampire warriors. Susan Elizabeth Phillips' Chicago Star series is about characters connected to a football team.

.   .   .

Theme

Another way to link a multi-protagonist series is through a theme. Janet Dailey's Americana series linked the books through the location, but also blended in the theme of America with a book set in each of the fifty US states. Sports romance is an entire sub-category that uses a theme to connect books.

You can also link a multi-protagonist series through a trope such as Jami Albright's Brides on the Run series. Anne Gracie uses a different romance trope in her Marriage of Convenience series.

BENEFITS OF A MULTI-PROTAGONIST SERIES

Probably the greatest benefit of this structure is its flexibility. You're not locked in to writing multiple books about a single protagonist. The loosely linked structure is ideal for a long series. If the series takes off, you can continue to write it, but add variation in characters and settings so that you don't become bored with it.

Because of the malleable structure, readers can drop in at different points. Perhaps they didn't enjoy one set of characters, but they may give another book a try because it revolves around another group of people or another location. Maybe a reader passed on the book about Joe in Montana (cowboys aren't her thing), but the

one about the billionaire who lives in New York is more
to her liking.

DRAWBACKS OF A MULTI-PROTAGONIST SERIES

Since you have a new protagonist with each book it may
take more time to write a new book than an author of a
single protagonist series, who writes the same protagonist in the same setting with familiar secondary
characters.

Multi-protagonist series aren't common in some
genres, so if you want to write this type of series you'll
probably find the most success in genres where this
structure is predominant, like romance. For instance,
cozy mystery readers want to return to the same protagonist in each book. They would probably skip over a
series with multiple protagonists because it's not what
they expect.

QUESTIONS: IF YOU'RE PLANNING A MULTI-PROTAGONIST SERIES

How will you link a multi-protagonist series?

Will you have an antagonist?

_____

_____

_____

_____

_____

_____

_____

How will the secondary characters take center stage in the following books?

_____

_____

_____

_____

_____

_____

_____

What is the setting? How will it appeal to fans of your genre? What sort of world-building do you need to do?

_____

_____

_____

_____

_____

_____

_____

What subplots will you have?

_____

_____

_____

_____

_____

_____

_____

How many books will be in your series initially?

_____

_____

_____

NOTES

_____

_____

_____

_____

_____

_____

_____

_____

_____

_____

_____

SINGLE PROTAGONIST SERIES

Jason Bourne. Hercule Poirot. Harry Potter. Jack Reacher. Anne Shirley. Frodo Baggins. Percy Jackson. Anne Shirley. Sherlock Holmes. Those character names bring to mind a rich fictional world with a single main character anchoring each book in the series. They're examples of the other type of series, the single protagonist series. The books center around the main character and their journey.

Jason Bourne is the protagonist of the Bourne series. The same goes for Anne Shirley even though those books have a completely different tone and setting. The protagonist is the focus of the series and carries the books. In every storyline, no matter how many books the series contains, the protagonist is the centerpiece, playing the main role and doing the heavy-lifting for the plot.

Growing up, Nancy Drew and Trixie Belden were some of my favorite books, so I was most familiar with the single protagonist series. However, I didn't realize the single protagonist series is broken down into two different types of protagonists: a protagonist with a flat character arc and a protagonist with a robust character arc. Let's look at the structure of each type of single protagonist series.

PROTAGONIST WITH A FLAT CHARACTER ARC

The flat character arc is actually an arc-less protagonist. Most of the craft advice for character development focuses on the main character's transformation. When the book ends, they've grown and changed—either in a positive or a negative way.

The flat arc character is the antithesis of the character who goes through a dramatic change. The flat arc character doesn't have a robust arc. They don't go through a massive transformative journey. A graph of their "arc" is closer to a horizontal line than a bell curve.

PROTAGONIST

Instead of going through the change themselves, the flat arc protagonist is the catalyst for change in the story world. Author and screenwriter Alexandra Sokoloff describes this situation as the Mysterious Stranger archetype in her book, *Screenwriting Tricks from Hollywood*.

Jack Reacher arrives, recognizes the problem, fixes the problem, and leaves town. James Bond does the same thing. He drops in, saves the world, and departs. Going from spy to spinster, Miss Marple also fits the pattern. She listens, asks questions, sorts out the murder, and then goes on with her life. She remains unchanged. It's the murderer and the people in St. Mary Mead who change.

Hercule Poirot is another example. He uses his little gray cells, flushes out the murderer and often brings love-lorn people together. Again, we have the main character land among a set of characters, he helps them work out their problems and produces change among the other characters, then he's on his way. Mary Poppins is another flat arc protagonist as is Katniss Everdeen.

Once I realized that there were protagonists with flat arcs, I understood why so much of the plotting and character advice I'd read often didn't fit seamlessly into a mystery plot. Mysteries, especially cozies, usually have a protagonist with a flat arc or a gentle curve of an arc, which was very different from the robust changes described in much of the writing craft advice on how to plot a novel.

K.M. Weiland describes the flat arc character as

already understanding the essential truth of the story that the other characters learn. Katniss knows "society should be based on trust and compassion, rather than fear and sadism."[1] She doesn't change her belief. She doesn't shift to a new belief as the story progresses. She acts in a way that transforms her world.

In a mystery, the arc-less sleuth pursues the truth, striving to reveal who the killer is, so equilibrium of the community can be restored. Knowing the truth of "who-dunit" won't change the sleuth's character, but it changes the world the sleuth lives in for the better.

In the thriller genre Jack Reacher is a prime example. Reacher remains the same. He values justice, and he brings vigilante justice to people who have escaped the official channels of the law.

ANTAGONIST

The antagonist may either be different with each book, or the same antagonist may appear throughout the series. Mysteries, especially those from the Golden Age of the 1920s and 1930s, generally have a different antagonist in each book. Poirot, Marple, and Lord Peter Wimsey expose the murderer and carry on to solve their next "case," which has a different antagonist.

Because the flat arc series character doesn't change dramatically, villains in this type of series are often more intriguing. Some of the most famous fictional villains are found in series with flat arc protagonists.

James Moriarty, Sherlock Holmes' nemesis, is a well-known example of an antagonist who carries on from book to book in a series with a flat arc protagonist.

The antagonist may be an organization that continually causes trouble for the protagonist, which is the case with Ian Fleming's creation of SMERSH. In the Jason Bourne series, it's the CIA that is the overarching antagonist. The head of the organization can be the ultimate villain of the series.

This structure creates an ideal situation where the author can increase the stakes throughout the series. In the early books, the protagonist deals with the agents of the organization, but as the stakes escalate throughout the series the protagonist struggles to identify the true mastermind, then confronts the head of the organization, the ultimate villain. It's a delicious layer cake of villainy for the author to explore and the reader to enjoy.

Other examples of an antagonist who appears in multiple books in a series with a flat arc protagonist are Count Olaf in *A Series of Unfortunate Events* and Sethos, the "master criminal" in Elizabeth Peters' Amelia Peabody series.

SETTING

The setting can be either fixed or variable. Miss Marple solved mysteries in St. Mary Mead, but she also traveled to London and other locations to solve crimes. James Bond found adventure all over the world. The important thing about setting and a flat arc protagonist is to meet genre expectations. Readers of a thriller like *The Da Vinci Code* expect a globe-trotting story, while a sci-fi series may be entirely set on a spaceship.

If the setting is limited in some way—perhaps it's in a confined geographic area such as a small town or village, or even a spaceship or space colony—consider what unique features (businesses, buildings, or the natural landscape) could support future novels in the series. How can you bring new characters and situations to the series? If it's a small town, does the town boom and become a bedroom community to a nearby larger town (built-in conflict in that scenario), or maybe a business relocates, bringing new jobs. Perhaps it's a college or tourist town with an influx of newcomers each semester or season.

SECONDARY CHARACTERS

As with the antagonist, the secondary characters in a series with a flat arc are often more interesting to readers because they're the characters who change and grow—or readers find them more relatable.

The brilliance of Sherlock and Poirot is hard to keep up with, and we identify with Watson and Hastings because sometimes we're as confused as the sidekicks are!

SUBPLOTS

A flat arc protagonist series can be episodic with no series-long subplots as is the case with mysteries from the Golden Age, or it can have a subplot that flows through the series. If a subplot runs throughout the series, it is often a conflict with a villain, as in the James Bond books.

POTENTIAL LENGTH OF FLAT ARC PROTAGONIST SERIES

A flat arc protagonist lends itself to a long series. It's much easier to create multiple story situations for a flat arc protagonist because the focus of the novel is on the story world rather than the main character. Jack Reacher, James Bond, and Hercule Poirot are examples. There's always more trouble for each one of these characters to sort out.

BENEFITS OF A FLAT ARC PROTAGONIST SERIES

This type of series structure allows you to create a long-running series. It works well with genres like mystery and thriller, which can have more "episodic" novels.

Christie could always bring a new client in for Poirot. There are enough problems in the world that need vigilante justice to keep Jack Reacher busy for a long time. Religious iconography, suspicious deaths, and historical cover-ups are the perfect set up for another Robert Langdon book.

DRAWBACKS OF A FLAT ARC PROTAGONIST SERIES

Modern readers tend to expect some sort of character arc, even if it's a small one. If the main character doesn't change at all, the series can feel static.

Since the secondary characters are often the ones changing in this type of series, they might outshine your protagonist. Or it might be the antagonist who steals the spotlight.

QUESTIONS: IF YOU'RE PLANNING A SERIES WITH A FLAT ARC PROTAGONIST

How will you make the main character interesting? How will you make sure the protagonist doesn't seem boring compared to the secondary characters and the antagonist?

_____

_____

_____

_____

_____

How will the secondary characters change around the protagonist?

_____

_____

_____

_____

_____

Will you have a single antagonist through the series or different ones in each book?

_____

_____

_____

_____

_____

_____

_____

What is the setting? How will it appeal to fans of your genre? How will the setting impact the series? Is it too limited?

_____

_____

_____

_____

_____

_____

_____

What world-building do you need to do?

_____

_____

_____

_____

_____

_____

_____

What subplots will you have? Will they flow throughout the series or be episodic?

_____

_____

_____

_____

_____

_____

_____

Does your series have an end-point or is it open-ended?

NOTES

PROTAGONIST WITH A ROBUST CHARACTER ARC

Now let's take a look at the other type of single protagonist structure, the series with a robust character arc. In a
series with a protagonist who has a robust character arc,
the main character goes through a tremendous change.
Because the protagonist is growing and changing, we
find them fascinating.

Jason Bourne is on a journey of self-discovery as he
tries to recover his memory. Percy Jackson and Harry
Potter struggle to understand and master their inherent
gifts while Frodo Baggins is on a literal quest as well as a
transformative journey of character growth.

I won't go into great depth about the different types
of robust character arcs because there is a wealth of
information and resources about that subject. What I
want to focus on is how the robust character arc fits

within a series. Instead of your protagonist completing his whole arc in one book, the protagonist with a robust character arc will be a thread that runs throughout the series.

Compare the character arc of Elizabeth Bennett with Harry Potter. Elizabeth comes to a greater self-awareness when she realizes she's misjudged Darcy. She says, "Till this moment I never knew myself." At the end of the book she's gained a deeper understanding of herself and of Darcy.

Harry Potter also changes dramatically, but his change is incremental. Like stepping-stones, Harry transforms from book to book. In the first book, he's unsure of himself and alone, ignorant of his power.

At the end of the first book in the Harry Potter series, *Harry Potter and the Sorcerer's Stone*, Harry has discovered he's a wizard and faced-off with Voldemort, although his mother's love and Dumbledore saved Harry. By the end of the series, Harry is confident and mature. He's developed a network of friends. He takes on and defeats Voldemort. He's a hero.

Elizabeth's character arc takes place in one novel, while Harry's takes place over a series of novels.

ANTAGONIST

The antagonist in the robust character arc series may be unique to each book, but often a single antagonist is woven into the series, providing a nemesis for the protagonist, as is the case with Voldemort. Other examples of antagonists in robust character arc series include Kronus in the Percy Jackson series and Sauron in the Lord of the Rings series. The antagonist may also be an organization, such as the CIA in the Jason Bourne series.

Similar to the antagonist in the series with a flat arc protagonist, the main character of the series may encounter lower-level agents or villains in the beginning of the series, but as the series nears its conclusion and the stakes rise, the protagonist works her way up the "food chain," facing bigger and bigger villains until she finally faces off with the ultimate antagonist, the one who's been the driving force behind the opposition to the protagonist all along.

SETTING

Like the flat arc protagonist series, you have many options when it comes to setting in a robust arc series. It can be fixed or variable, but should reflect reader expectations. One of the draws of sci-fi and fantasy is the exploration of new and unusual worlds and creatures, while mystery readers love to get to know a small town or village intimately.

Jason Bourne travels the world, but Harry Potter's story takes place mostly in a school. Like the setting of a flat arc protagonist series, you'll want to consider how the setting will impact the series.

SECONDARY CHARACTERS

In a robust arc series, secondary characters may have strong arcs of their own. At the beginning of the Harry Potter series, Hermione is a bookish know-it-all, but by the final book she's matured into a wise young woman who is secure and doesn't need to show-off.

Secondary characters can also act as foils, or mirrors, for the protagonist. In the Anne of Green Gables series, Diana Barry is the opposite of Anne Shirley not only in appearance but also in personality. Anne dislikes her red hair and freckles, but considers Diana with her dark hair and porcelain complexion pretty. While Anne is vivacious and bold, Diana is less imaginative and a follower.

SUBPLOTS

Subplots in a series with a robust protagonist can be complex and layered. You can have subplots related to the series arc as well as subplots related to the main character.

Additionally, you may have subplots about secondary characters that flow throughout the series. For example, in the Harry Potter series, Harry has a robust arc, the secondary characters of Ron and Hermione have arcs, and there is a series arc involving Voldemort, not to mention several mystery subplots that are also threaded throughout the series.

LENGTH

The length of the robust arc series is often determined by the arc of the protagonist, which means that this type of series can be more limiting than a series with a flat arc protagonist.

Once the ring in The Lord of the Rings is destroyed, the quest is accomplished. Once Harry has matured and vanquished Voldemort, the story is over. It would be hard to continue either of these series without launching a new arc, which is what some authors do, and we'll delve into that option in the Troubleshooting chapter.

BENEFITS OF A ROBUST PROTAGONIST

You can create a strong bond between the reader and the protagonist with a robust arc. Readers are invested in the main character's journey and look forward to each new book.

DRAWBACKS OF A ROBUST PROTAGONIST

This structure has a build-in end point: when the protagonist reaches the end of their journey, you have a natural conclusion. It can be hard to extend this type of series beyond the natural end-point.

QUESTIONS: IF YOU'RE PLANNING A SERIES WITH A ROBUST ARC PROTAGONIST

How does the protagonist change in each book as well as over the course of the series?

Will any secondary characters have a strong arc?

Are any secondary characters foils/mirrors of the protagonist?

Will you have a single antagonist through the series or different ones in each book?

What is the setting? How will it appeal to fans of your genre? How will the setting impact the series? What world-building do you need to do?

_____

_____

_____

_____

_____

_____

_____

What subplots will you have? Will they flow throughout the series or be confined to each book?

_____

_____

_____

_____

_____

_____

What is the end point of your protagonist's arc? Will that be the end of the series? How can you extend the series if you'd like to continue writing it after the initial arc is complete?

QUESTIONS: IF YOU'RE NOT SURE WHICH TYPE OF SERIES YOU SHOULD USE

Which is most common for your genre, multi-protagonist or single protagonist series? List examples of popular series in your genre as a jumping-off point for brainstorming your series.

Which type of series appeals to you most, one with multiple protagonists or one with a single protagonist? Why?

_____

_____

_____

_____

_____

_____

_____

If you're considering a single protagonist series, which type of arc would be best for your character, flat or robust?

_____

_____

_____

_____

_____

Once you've decided on a series type, what are the draw-backs or challenges you might need to deal with?

_____

_____

_____

_____

_____

_____

_____

NOTES

CRAFTING YOUR SERIES

Once you've decided on the structure of your series, you'll have a variety of choices in the way you put it together. In this section we'll look at ways you can use character arcs and subplots to create series cohesion and draw readers from book to book.

Then we'll consider how many books you want for your series and common patterns of arrangement. Finally, we'll delve into endings and connections: how to end a series, how to connect multiple series into literary universes, and how to extend a series.

CHARACTER ARCS AND SUBPLOTS

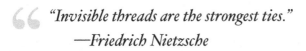 *"Invisible threads are the strongest ties."*
—*Friedrich Nietzsche*

Character arcs and subplots are the most powerful structural elements you can use to link the books in your series.

CHARACTER ARCS

When you create a character arc that flows from book to book, you give your reader a strong incentive to read through the series. Whether you're using a robust arc protagonist or a flat arc protagonist you can still create arcs that pull readers from book to book.

Each book must be a complete and satisfying story, but when you overlay the extra arc that runs throughout all the books, you give the series more depth and make it more compelling to your readers.

ROBUST ARC PROTAGONIST SERIES

A protagonist with a robust arc will change incrementally. Each book must be a complete arc of its own, so you have a structure of smaller arcs within the larger arc of the series.

You could use the Hero's Journey to structure the overall arc of your series, with each book focusing on a specific part of the journey. The primary arc of Book One could be about the Call to Adventure, Book Two could focus on meeting a mentor and training, Book Three could center on facing Trials and Challenges, Book Four's storyline could be about the descent into the Abyss, Book Five could trace the Transformation of the Hero, who now has a new perspective, and Book Six could detail the Final Battle and Return.

The Hero's Journey is just one way to structure your series. Other potential character arcs are:

- Romance
- Healing

- Self-awareness
- Atonement
- Revenge
- Justice
- Truth
- Discovery
- Fall from Grace
- Maturity
- Forgiveness

FLAT ARC PROTAGONIST SERIES

Flat Arc Protagonist series usually won't have a dramatic transformation in the protagonist, but you can include character arcs. Most likely these arcs will focus on the secondary characters. You can use the potential arcs listed in the section above to spark ideas for your secondary character's arcs.

In the section on the drawbacks of writing a flat arc protagonist series, I mentioned that modern readers often expect some sort of character arc, even if it's a small one. If your protagonist never changes at all, the series can feel static.

One way to keep your protagonist from feeling stuck is to give them small arcs or challenges. These lower-key elements don't overpower the storyline, but give your protagonist room to change in subtle ways. Check out the section on dealing with Stuck Characters in the

Trouble Shooting chapter for tips on adding small arcs and challenges.

SUBPLOTS

Subplots, smaller stories within the large story, are another element that can flow throughout your series and pull readers from book to book.

Romantic

The romantic subplot is one of the most common types of subplots and can be found in most genres. If you spinout the romance over the course of a series, that's a strong draw to pull readers to the next book.

A love triangle can be an even bigger draw as readers root for their favorite and eagerly pick up the next book to see the progress of the relationship. A problem can develop if the love triangle drags on after readers expect a resolution. The Troubleshooting chapter explores the problems and possible solutions to a stuck love triangle.

Revenge

Moving from love to hate, a revenge subplot could power your series, particularly as a motivation for your antagonist. Or you could flip it around and have a revenge subplot motivate your main character.

. . .

Economic

An economic subplot has more to do with the setting than the characters. Perhaps the series takes place in a city that's trying to revitalize its downtown. The subplot could follow the city's progress and setbacks. Will the venture work and rejuvenate the city?

Entrepreneurial

An entrepreneurial subplot could follow a person who starts or inherits a business. Will they be successful in the new venture?

Environmental

A subplot could center on the environment, especially in sci-fi or post-apocalyptic sub-genres. Will your characters learn how to survive in the new environment? Or will they try to escape to a safer environment?

Mentor

A subplot about a mentor could focus on the growth of the main character as they learn from the mentor, then perhaps the protagonist reaches a point where they must save the mentor—or the mentor turns on the protégé.

Shadow Governing Council

A controlling government-type agency (usually behind-the-scenes) is a popular subplot that's often found in thrillers as well as sci-fi. The protagonist must first discover the existence of the hidden ruling agency, then defeat it, preventing some sort of calamity.

QUESTIONS

What character arcs appeal to you from the ones listed in this section?

_____

_____

_____

_____

_____

_____

_____

Can you think of other arcs?

_____

_____

_____

_____

_____

_____

_____

Which arcs will you use in your series?

_____

_____

_____

_____

_____

_____

_____

What subplots appeal to you from the ones listed in this section?

_____

_____

_____

_____

_____

_____

Can you think of other subplots?

_____

_____

_____

_____

_____

_____

What subplots do you often see in your genre?

_____

_____

_____

_____

_____

_____

_____

Which subplots will you use in your series?

_____

_____

_____

_____

_____

_____

_____

NOTES

SERIES PATTERNS

Now that we've covered the different types of series and compelling ways to link your series through character arcs and subplots, let's focus on the overall structure of the series.

Fortunately, a series can take many different forms, so you're not locked into a single arrangement. Some of the popular series patterns are: duet, trilogy, linked trilogy, and open-ended.

DUET

The duet pattern is popular in romance. It's a good way to test a series idea. If the series idea proves popular, you can extend the series later. On the other hand, some stories don't lend themselves to a long series. Two books may be all you need to explore a story idea.

TRILOGY

A trilogy is the most popular series structure. Some of the most famous series books are trilogies: The Lord of the Rings series, The Hunger Games series, the Fifty Shades series, the Twilight series, the Bourne series, and His Dark Materials series, to name just a few. It's not surprising this pattern of three related things is so popular.

We love this pattern and see it over and over again. From nursery rhymes (*Three Little Pigs* and *Three Blind Mice*) to religious associations (Father, Son, and Holy Spirit) to plotting (Three Act Structure), threes are everywhere.

A series about three friends or three sisters or three locations appeals to us, probably because the pattern is so ingrained in our collective psyche. Alexandra Sokoloff has a terrific post that explores the "Rule of Three," if you want more examples.[1]

LINKED TRILOGY

The linked trilogy is a pattern of 3 + 3. The first three books have an arc, as do the next three, and so on, but there is usually an overarching arc to the whole series as well. One of the advantages of this type of series is that if the first three books don't do well, you can wrap up the overarching series arc in the third book and end the series there. That way you don't have frustrated readers longing for a series conclusion.

Almost any genre can use this series pattern, and it can be as complex or as simple as you like. A sci-fi series might have the first three books center on the effort to get a crippled ship to a planet where the characters can survive, the next three books might focus on the difficulties of surviving on the new planet and efforts to repair the ship, and then the next three books might be about the journey in the repaired ship to their original destination. Or you might have an even grander scale with a series that revolves around inter-galaxy wars that take place over millennia.

I'm using this pattern in my High Society Lady Detective historical mystery series, but it's a much simpler framework. The first three books, set in the 1920s, are about Olive discovering she's good at detecting as she works for family and friends. The next three books are about her creating a business, establishing an office and building her reputation as a detective. In the next three books, clients will seek out Olive.

WARNING ABOUT ENDING A SERIES EARLY

Subplots are unresolved questions that pull readers from book to book through the series. Will Abby finally get pregnant after years of infertility? Will the restaurant in the small town be a success? Will Olive and Jasper become a couple? Notice that these aren't the major story question. (Olive and Jasper are characters in a mystery, not a romance!)

The major story question must be resolved in a satisfying way for readers, but these smaller threads and open questions keep readers thinking about your story and keep them on the lookout for more books.

If you're not sure if you want to write the next book, don't leave any subplots unresolved. Close those loops. Otherwise, you'll have upset readers—and rightfully so. You promised them a certain experience and hinted there was more to come, then left them hanging. That's not a good reading experience, and they'll be less likely to try more of your books.

In fact, many readers won't pick up a series unless they know it's complete. They've been burned too many times by authors who started a series, then dropped it without providing a satisfying conclusion.

QUESTIONS

Which series pattern will you use? Why?

_____

_____

_____

_____

_____

_____

What subplots will you use to pull readers through the series?

_____

_____

_____

_____

_____

_____

If you need to cut the series short, can you end it early? How will you wrap up the subplots and open threads in a satisfying way for the reader at an earlier point than you originally planned?

NOTES

_____

_____

_____

_____

_____

_____

_____

_____

_____

_____

_____

_____

CLIFFHANGERS AND READ-THROUGH HOOKS

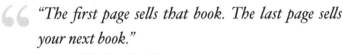 *"The first page sells that book. The last page sells your next book."*
— *Mickey Spillane*

Now let's consider endings of the individual novels in a series and look at two different ways to handle the finale of books within a series: cliffhangers and read-through hooks.

CLIFFHANGERS

There are two important things to know about cliffhangers. One, readers say they hate them. Two, cliffhangers give authors good read-through rates. I don't know of any scientific studies I can site here, but I do know the consensus among authors is that despite readers disliking (sometimes despising) cliffhangers, a cliffhanger can lead to readers who are anxious for the next book in the series.

A cliffhanger is a plot that isn't resolved. According to The Online Etymology Dictionary, the word developed to describe the endings of serialized movies from the silent era, such as the *Perils of Pauline*, which were episodic. The entry quotes *Colliers* magazine, which described how the episodes often ended with the heroine "hanging over a cliff from a fraying rope through which the villain was sawing with a dull knife. . ."[1]

Your reader began reading the book with the expectation that the plotline would be resolved, but it wasn't. You snipped the narrative thread, ending the book without fulfilling your reader's expectation, which is why some readers won't ever read another book from an author who publishes a book with a cliffhanger.

This story-telling technique works well for serialized content like episodic shows, but it can cause friction between book authors and readers when it's used in novels. Generally, there's a longer time between the release of a novel compared to a show—months or years, instead of days or weeks, which is the cause of readers' frustration. They don't want to wait that long to find out what happens.

Of course you'll always have readers who have been burned and refuse to read a book with a cliffhanger, so if you use them you risk ticking off a certain portion of readers. However, it seems that despite the fact that readers find them annoying, most readers do go on to read the next book instead of abandoning the series.

Because there's a chance you can lose readers, cliffhangers need a "use with caution" sign. The best-case scenario for a cliffhanger would be if the next book in the series is either released immediately or out after a short wait. Another option would be to have the next book on preorder. All three of these situations signal to the reader that they'll be able to continue the story and find out what happens.

READ-THROUGH HOOKS

A hook is a narrative device placed at the end of the story. After the plot of the book is resolved, a hook gives readers a glimpse of the next book. Like the samples you can try at the grocery store, you're giving your reader a little taste of what's to come.

I've had success using read-through hooks in the High Society Lady Detective series. At the end of the second book in the series, *Murder at Blackburn Hall*, Olive receives a letter from a woman asking for help in sorting out some rumors about a mummy curse that's plaguing her family. It's a little preview of the next book,

The Egyptian Antiquities Murder, which was on preorder. I had an all-time high number of preorders on that book. It worked so well that I included a read-through hook at the end of the Egyptian book and plan to continue to use them in the series. Read-through hooks are easy to use in the historical mystery series because each book is a new case for Olive to solve, but you could use read-through hooks in all types of series as long as you know enough about the next book to create a compelling hook for it.

Another example of a read-through hook is Clair's revelation at the end of *Outlander* that she's pregnant. Rick Riordan uses read-through hooks extensively in the Heroes of Olympus series, with almost every book ending with a hint of what the next book will be about.

QUESTIONS

List the books that you waited anxiously for the next book in the series. What sort of endings did the author use?

_____

_____

_____

What sort of endings will the individual books in your series have? Will you use a cliffhanger? Why or why not?

What kind of read-through hook could you use at the end of each book to give your reader a taste of the next one?

NOTES

_____

_____

_____

_____

_____

_____

_____

_____

_____

_____

_____

_____

ENDING A SERIES

How do you know it's time to end a series? For some series, the answer is easy. If you're writing a robust character arc series and the character arc is complete, then the series has a natural ending point, as is the case with the Harry Potter series.

Life transitions such as leaving college, getting married, or retiring from a job often provide natural ending points for character arcs. On the other hand, a flat arc series is structured so that it can go on indefinitely, but you may decide it's time to end a series.

SIGNS IT MIGHT BE TIME TO END YOUR SERIES

You're bored with your protagonist. Like Sir Arthur Conan Doyle, you may be tired of the character and feel limited.

You're having trouble coming up with story ideas. Maybe you've explored all of the themes and storylines you envisioned and can't come up with an idea large enough to carry a novel.

Read-through isn't strong. A series is like a funnel. Many readers will try the first book, but only a portion of those will go on to read Book Two. Hopefully most of your readers who loved the second book will go on to read the next and then continue through the series.

If you're not seeing strong read-through, then you're dealing with the law of diminishing returns. If you continue to release more books but your audience is getting smaller with each book, it might make more sense to end the series and start fresh.

Reader reviews are lack-luster. If you see descriptions complaining the books "aren't as good as they used to be" then it might be time to wrap up a series. If you continue writing a series that you don't feel passionate about, it can actually harm your writing career. If you're not excited about writing a book, it may come through in the story.

If a reader picks up your new release from late in a series and doesn't have a good reading experience, then it may put them off from ever trying another one of your books. Or you may lose faithful readers. How many times have you heard readers say (either in person or in reviews), "I stopped reading that author. Their books just aren't good anymore."

ANXIETY AROUND ENDING A SERIES

Why do we have so much angst about ending a series? An ending is a change and any change can be stressful. Let's look at the issues around ending a series—some practical and some emotional—and see how we can reduce our stress.

Investment of Time and Money

We've invested time and creative energy in crafting a series, not to mention the effort and money we put into promoting the books. Financially, ending a series can be a risk. If a series is earning money, will ending it lead to a downturn in your revenue?

If you've decided the best approach is to end the series, then this is a mindset issue. Instead of worrying about what you might lose, refocus your thoughts on how the completed series can work for you. It's now part of your backlist. It can continue to earn money even if you don't add new books to it.

With strategic sales and other promotions you can revive interest in it. Some readers hold off on reading a series until it's complete, so use that detail to your advantage. In your marketing play up the fact that the series is finished. Check out the Marketing chapter for more ideas. Remember that traditional publishers have used the technique of marketing their older books for years. Their backlist is their bread-and-butter. You can follow the same model.

Loyalty

There's an emotional component to our anxiety as well. We're attached to the characters, and ending a series can almost feel disloyal, as if we're abandoning the characters.

This is another mindset issue. Only a creative would worry about the feelings of a character! Sometimes I have to give myself a stern talking-to and remind myself that I'm writing about *fictional* characters, and I'm not being disloyal if I end a series. (Yes, I'm weird!)

Reader Reaction

Then there's the readers to consider. If we've done

our job well, readers are attached to the story world. They don't want to see the series end. They'll lobby for more books and, as someone who doesn't like to disappoint anyone, I find it hard to squash the people-pleaser in me and say "no" to readers. The reality is that if readers love a series, they're never going to be happy if you end it. They'll always want more books, but that's a good thing. This is another mindset shift.

Instead of focusing on the negative (*they're so disappointed*) realize you've done your job well and created passionate readers. You can use the opportunity to connect with your readers and move them on to another series, which we'll look at in the next chapter on spinoffs and literary universes.

HOW TO TELL YOUR READERS

When you end a series, you can take one of two approaches: quietly let it die or be upfront about it.

The quiet approach

When I decided I wouldn't write any more Ellie books, I ended the series quietly. I focused my newsletter and my social media on the new series I was working on. When readers asked if there would be more books in the Ellie series I explained that I wasn't currently working on more books in the series at that time. I was reluctant to completely close the door on that character and series. Eventually, I came to terms with ending the series and updated my readers in my newsletter.

I told them I had no more plans for books in that series. Ellie and her family were in a good place. They were raising their kids and living life without finding any dead bodies. I also explained that I didn't want the series to go stale and that I didn't have ideas that would support a whole novel. Many readers replied to let me know they'd miss Ellie, but they didn't like a series to go downhill and could understand the decision.

The upfront approach

When it comes to ending a series, the other option is to announce it upfront. You can use the last book in the series to transition readers to another series. I've taken this approach with the end of my On the Run series.

The final book, *Duplicity*, is a crossover book with a dual timeline. Modern-day art recovery specialist Zoe is researching the history of a painting. The second storyline is about Olive from the High Society Lady Detective series and her search for the painting when it went missing in 1923.

The back matter of the book announces that *Duplicity* is the last planned book in the On the Run series. I hope interweaving the two timelines will give readers a taste of my other series and will draw some over to the newer series. Crossover books are just one way to transition readers to a new series. We'll look at other ways to connect series, including spinoffs and literary universes, next.

QUESTIONS

List the book series that you've lost interest in. Why did you stop reading them?

List the book series that ended in a satisfying way. What did you like about the endings? Why were they satisfying?

_____

_____

_____

_____

_____

What issues around ending a series do you struggle with? Are they mechanical or mindset issues? If they're mechanical, make a list of topics to research to help you with the craft aspects. If they're mindset, how will you transition your thinking?

_____

_____

_____

_____

_____

_____

If you have to end a series, which approach to telling your readers appeals to you? Why?

_____

_____

_____

_____

_____

_____

_____

NOTES

_____

_____

_____

_____

_____

_____

_____

_____

_____

_____

_____

_____

CONNECTING SERIES: SPINOFFS AND LITERARY UNIVERSES

> " "*Don't adventures ever have an end? I suppose not. Someone else always has to carry on the story.*"
> —*J.R.R. Tolkien*

If you can connect an existing series to a new series your readers will probably be more willing to give the new series a try.

Connecting series is like leveling up. Instead of linking individual books, now you're linking groups of books, which can be powerful for increasing your reader loyalty as well as read-through.

CHARACTER SPINOFFS

You can write a crossover book as I mentioned previously, or you can simply spinoff a single character and create a new book or series that's related to the original series. *The Adventures of Huckleberry Finn* is a spinoff from *The Adventures of Tom Sawyer*.

LITERARY UNIVERSES

When you create a spinoff character and give them their own book or series, you're creating a literary universe that's bigger than just one series.

Rick Riodian's The Heroes of Olympus is a spinoff from Percy Jackson and The Olympians. The spinoff series took some of the secondary characters, like Annabeth, from the original series and made them point of view characters in the new series. The original series explored Greek mythology, while the spinoff series combined Greek and Roman mythology. Other spinoffs in the universe went on to explore Egyptian as well as Norse mythology.

An example of a literary universe from the indie publishing world is Michael Anderle's Kurtherian Gambit universe, which has multiple series connected to it, but sprawling literary universes have been around a long time. *The Hobbit* and its follow-up series, *The Lord of the Rings* explored the literary universe of Middle-earth.

Issac Asimov wrote several different science fiction series, including the Foundation series, the Galactic Empire series, and the Robot series, which were all linked through the same literary universe, but the books ranged along a timeline that spanned thousands of years.

While massive literary universes are frequently found in sci-fi and fantasy, you can have a literary universe in other genres as well. I've created a literary universe around an English village. Nether Woodsmoor, my fictional Derbyshire village with the nearby stately home of Parkview Hall is the setting for the Murder on Location series, a cozy mystery series with a contemporary setting.

When I decided to write a historical mystery series set in England in the 1920s, I linked the two series by having the main character of the historical series grow up in Nether Woodsmoor and be a relative of the owners of Parkview Hall.

A literary universe gives readers several entry points to your series. They may find you through Book One of your original series. Or they may begin with a spinoff series. If they love the books, they'll probably want to go back and read the original series, especially if it has some of the same characters in it.

Having multiple entry points to your literary world means you're not locked into a single entry point at Book One of the series, which may be a weaker book since your writing has probably improved over time.

COMPANION BOOKS

If you create a literary universe you can add to it not only through series books but also through companion books, which are books that explore certain aspects of the stories in more depth. They may not fit within a novel, but readers are interested in these side stories.

Fantastic Beasts and Where to Find Them is a textbook that was mentioned in the Harry Potter series. Published after the conclusion of the series, the guidebook lists the beasts within the Harry Potter universe and it's spawned a movie series.

The Percy Jackson series has a companion book, *Demigods and Monsters,* as well as *The Demigod Diaries,* which features short stories and character interviews.

RETELLINGS

We can't leave the subject of literary universes without touching on literary retellings, which tell the story of a well-known literary figure, setting, or universe with a new twist, often with a revisionist slant.

Longbourn is a retelling of *Pride and Prejudice* from the point of view of the servants. The novel *Wicked* put a new spin on The *Wizard of Oz*, reimagining the story of the Wicked Witch of the West.

A retelling may be genre-crossing as in the parody

novel, *Pride, Prejudice, and Zombies. Cinder* is a retelling of Cinderella that mixes a fairy tale with sci-fi.

Multiple Retellings from the Same Literary Universe

Sometimes a literary universe is so fertile that it produces multiple retellings. The world of Sherlock Holmes is a prime example of this phenomenon.

There are fictional series with retellings featuring Moriarty, Mrs. Hudson, and Mycroft Holmes as protagonists. Another series imagines Holmes in retirement as he mentors a young protege, Mary Russell. Sherry Thomas writes a gender-flip retelling with Sherlock as a woman. Brittany Cavallaro's Charlotte Holmes series is another gender-flip that explores the idea of descendants of Holmes and Watson working together. The Brothers of Baker Street series features two brothers who work out of an office located at 221B Baker Street and have to deal with the mail that is still delivered to Sherlock Holmes.

Benefits and Drawbacks of Retellings

Writing a retelling of a famous literary work has the benefit of a built-in audience. Holmes fans are hungry for more stories in the universe, but that also means there's lots of competition in the Holmes retelling category.

You'll probably have noticed that all the retellings mentioned here are based on literary works that have fallen out of copyright, an essential factor to consider if you'd like to write a retelling.

Creating a series that links to a popular established fictional character or world can be an effective strategy for launching a series, but you need a unique take on the original content.

QUESTIONS

List your favorite spinoff characters. What do you love about them?

List the spinoff characters that didn't work for you. Why didn't they appeal to you?

_____

_____

_____

_____

_____

_____

_____

What characters could you spinoff from your series?

_____

_____

_____

_____

_____

_____

_____

What literary universes do you enjoy? What is it about them that appeals to you?

_____

_____

_____

_____

_____

_____

_____

How could you expand your series into a literary universe?

_____

_____

_____

_____

_____

_____

_____

What companion books could you create to further expand your literary universe?

_____

_____

_____

_____

_____

_____

If your series is a retelling, what unique spin will you put on the original material? Will your take appeal to readers of the original?

_____

_____

_____

_____

_____

_____

NOTES

EXTENDING A SERIES

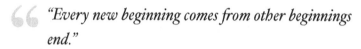 *"Every new beginning comes from other beginnings end."*

—*Seneca*

In certain situations you may decide you don't want to end a series, launch a spinoff, or expand the literary universe. You may decide you want to extend a series.

Extending a series can be tricky. If you've written a robust arc and your protagonist has come to the end of the arc, then you'll need something to relaunch the main character on a new arc.

I was in this situation when I came to the end of Book Four in my On the Run series. I'd originally planned to write a trilogy with Zoe searching for her missing ex who'd become embroiled in a financial scandal. In the first book Zoe was trying to find out if he was really dead (spoiler, he wasn't!), then the next two books they untangled the conspiracy that had set him up as a fall guy. By the end of Book Three, Jack had been cleared and the romantic subplot was resolved with Jack proposing and Zoe accepting. My readers loved the series and asked for more books. I thought, *I can write one more book, a honeymoon book*, which I did, *Suspicious*.

The central premise of the first books in the series was that Jack was on the run and I knew I couldn't keep him continually on the run no matter how much my readers wanted more books, so Book Four would be the end of the series. But then as I wrote the final chapters I saw a way to continue the series.

The insurance recovery specialist who had been dogging their steps offered Zoe a job as a consultant. With that simple change, the series could continue with themes about Zoe solving her first art recovery case. Subsequent books explored how Zoe established herself as an art recovery specialist. She and Jack weren't on the run anymore; they were pursuing the bad guys who were on the run after stealing valuable art and antiquities.

TIPS FOR EXTENDING A SERIES

Find a logical extension of the original story line

Your protagonist discovers the antagonist was just the first level antagonist, and there's a bigger, badder antagonist. Or your protagonist faces a new challenge, like the one described above.

Once Zoe discovered the true story about Jack's background and they'd cleared his name, she takes on a new job in loss recovery that makes use of her new skills. Make sure you avoid repeating the old arc so that it doesn't feel like the characters are just looping through the same storyline again.

Weaving in a new subplot can extend a series. Some common subplots:

- Romantic subplot—a little romance is usually a winner with readers, no matter what the genre.
- Secret identity—either that of your main character of a secondary character. The element of mystery is one way to keep readers going from book to book.
- Quest—for a physical thing or something intangible, like a lost spell.
- Entrepreneurial/Career—climbing the

corporate ladder or establishing a successful
business has inherent ups and downs, which
are ideal for plotting and complicating your
protagonist's world.

- Personal growth—An example of this type of
subplot would be a character reconnecting
with an estranged family member. Or it could
be a "buddy" subplot with your main
character establishing a deeper friendship.

Wipe the slate clean

You can also give your characters or world a reset,
but this can be a risky tactic. If you're writing a para-
normal world, you have the ability to literally revive dead
characters, which could give you all sorts of complica-
tions and new storylines.

If you're writing in a more "real world" setting,
perhaps your character was only assumed to be dead.
Doyle brought Sherlock back with the explanation that
Sherlock had faked his own death. There are problems
with resurrecting characters. Readers who mourned a
character's death may be more annoyed than delighted
to see a character reappear.

A less risky way to employ this tactic is to bring back
a character who "went off the page." If you had someone

move away or go away to college or travel to a different city, it's much easier to bring that character back.

Other options include memory troubles. Amnesia, memory wipes, or mental issues all could give a series a new direction, but handle these with care, especially amnesia, which can stray into the ridiculous if you're not careful.

Depending on your genre, you may be able to literally change your character. Perhaps a human becomes a vampire. Or in a less dramatic and more reality-based genre where you can't transform your protagonist to another creature, what if you change their work life? What if a thief reforms? Or what if a cop retires? A shift in a character's personal life (a couple has a baby, a couple divorces, or two divorced people remarry) can add new subplots and storylines.

If you decide to wipe the slate clean and start over, make sure you don't remove the elements your readers enjoy. If a small town is the draw of your series, don't move your protagonist to the big city.

QUESTIONS

How could you extend your original storyline?

_____

_____

_____

_____

_____

What new subplot could you add to your original story to give it new life?

_____

_____

_____

_____

_____

_____

Do any aspects of your genre tropes or conventions give you ideas for reviving the series?

_____

_____

_____

_____

_____

_____

What could you do to give your characters a reset?

_____

_____

_____

_____

_____

_____

NOTES

PRACTICALITIES

Whew, you've made some of the hard decisions about your series—or at least created a plan to start with. Now it's time to get practical and think about the writing itself and problems that might crop up.

We'll take a look at batch writing and troubleshoot common problems that come up when writing a series.

BATCH WRITING

If you're writing a series, batch writing can save you time and help with continuity. I recently tried batch-writing books and now I'm a fan of it. I'd always written a book, put it through the post-production cycle of copy-edits, proofreading, and formatting, then released it before moving on to the next book. Once that book was out, I'd repeat the cycle.

With my historical mystery series, I decided to try writing the first three books back-to-back. I wrote the first two books in the High Society Lady Detective series, then sent them to my copy editor. I worked on the third book while waiting on the edits.

CONTINUITY

Writing the books consecutively helped with continuity. After I finished the second book, I realized there were details I needed to change in the first book. The same thing happened with Book Three. Because I hadn't actually published any of the books I was able to fine-tune the plot and make changes to the series.

In fact, I actually moved the setting of the books. I'd originally written Book One with a setting in 1922, but I moved it a year later because in the third book I wanted to explore the interest in Egypt after King Tut's tomb was opened in 1923.

Staying in the same story world also helped keep the plotlines and characters fresh in my mind. I didn't have to go back and look for small details like the name of the neighbor or someone's eye color or height. The books were top-of-mind, which saved me time while I was writing.

Writing in the same story world without taking a break also helped me with plotting. I need "thinking time" when I immerse myself in the world of the story as I work out the plot. Since my thoughts were already in Olive's world, it didn't take me as long to figure out the details for the subsequent books.

An interesting aspect of the process of batch writing is that the novels are tightly interconnected. The books of the series are much closer together on the timeline than any of my other series. Since I'm using read-through hooks at the end of the books, the story flows from one book to the next with little time in between. It gives the series a completely different feel from my other books.

With my other series, I took a break between each book, so when I came back to the series it "felt" as if time had gone by, and I set the next book a few months after the previous one. In the High Society series, the books are only a few weeks—or in some cases, a few days—apart in "book time."

Of course, you don't have to batch-write a series. If your system is write-release-write and it's working for you, keep at it! If you want to try batch writing, then writing several books in the same series would be a good way to test the process.

QUESTIONS

If you're interested in batch-writing, do you have time in your production schedule to write several books back-to-back?

_____

_____

_____

If you need to make adjustments to your schedule, how will you do that?

_____

_____

_____

_____

_____

_____

_____

Can you afford to bank the books and hold them until you have several finished?

_____

_____

_____

_____

_____

_____

_____

NOTES

TROUBLESHOOTING

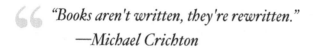

"Books aren't written, they're rewritten."
—*Michael Crichton*

Most problems with a series fall into one of two categories. The first type of problem is something technical like structure, which can be solved in a straightforward way—learning a new aspect of the craft or mastering a certain skill related to series writing. The other type of problem falls into the category of mindset.

TECHNICAL ISSUES

REINTRODUCING CHARACTERS AND SITUATIONS IN LATER BOOKS

Even if your read-through from book to book is strong you'll still need to reintroduce characters from previous books as well as significant events that happened in previous books. Although some readers prefer to begin a series with the first book, other readers will pick up any book in the series and they'll be unfamiliar with the backstory of the previous books. Even your core readers may have forgotten some details and a quick reminder will refresh their memory.

The trick is to give just enough information to bring the reader up to speed, but not so much that the section drags down the narrative. A quick summary is what you want, and if you integrate the refresh with the protagonist's current world, all the better.

Here's an example from the second book in the High Society Lady Detective series, *Murder at Blackburn Hall.*

I couldn't quite believe it had come to this, applying for jobs again. After what happened at Archly Manor, I'd been so sure I was on my way.

I'd taken a job and completed it successfully. I was the first to admit the route to the conclusion had taken a few rather unusual turns—hairpin turns, to be completely accurate. But I'd done it. And been paid, too. I'd returned to London with enough money to pay the rent on my pokey room and even repair my motor, a dear little Morris Cowley, and garage it in London.

But my funds were dwindling at a rapid rate. My choices were either to go back to the job search, or return to live in Tate House with my father and Sonia. I'd rather model hats for every snobbish high society matron in London than live under my new stepmother's thumb.

The short section lets readers know Olive was involved in another mystery at Archly Manor, but doesn't reveal any details or spoilers. Additionally, it gives an insight into Olive's independent character, and it reveals she has a strained relationship with her new stepmother.

JUGGLING A LARGE CAST OF SECONDARY CHARACTERS

If you have a long series you'll have an ever-growing cast of secondary characters. As your cast balloons in size, one way to prevent stories from becoming overloaded is to focus the narrative on a few characters in each book.

Every character doesn't have to appear in every book. In my Ellie Avery series some of the books focused on her life as a military spouse and those books featured characters at the squadron, but other books centered on her extended Southern family. The quirky relatives showed up in the family-focused books, but not the military-focused books.

Another way to handle a large cast is to send some of the characters off the page for a book or two. Perhaps a daughter goes away to college or a friend leaves town for a time to visit a relative. A secondary character might take a consulting job in another state. Or in a sci-fi series, a character might leave to explore another planet or galaxy.

IMMUTABILITY

Immutability can be a problem for series writers. Once you've described something—a person's age or a physical location of a building or how the magic system works—you're locked in.

• *Generalities*

I've learned generalities can be my friend. Specific

details are wonderful when it comes to descriptions, but I try to limit irrelevant details now. For instance, I'd rather say someone is in their early twenties instead of twenty-two years old. That generality gives me some wiggle room if I want or need to slightly shift their age one way or the other in a future book. If I don't need to be specific for the story, I'd use "several months ago," instead of "five months ago."

Sci-fi and fantasy writers have some leeway because they have the option of creating rules for their world, but readers like consistency. Don't break the rules of your world just to make a plot point work.

Technology changes fast. What's cutting edge today can make your books feel dated in a few years. I wish I hadn't described my character "flipping her phone closed" in my early books. Now I try to avoid verbiage that might date my books. Instead of describing someone "swiping open" or "scrolling down," I'll limit myself to "he called her," or "she searched for X."

• *Think Ahead*

As you write, try to keep the long view in mind. If your thriller protagonist has a pet, how does that impact the series? Does she have to rush home to let the dog out after work? Or will you create a considerate neighbor who helps her take the dog for a walk or feed the cat?

What about kids in your story? How fast will they age? Who will take care of them when your protagonist is out saving the world or falling in love?

If you give your protagonist a sister, what impact does that have on the series? How involved will the character be in the story and in future books in the series? She's related to the protagonist, so readers may expect to see her in other books. If it's a multi-protagonist series, will readers want to read the sister's story, too? This situation could be a positive, if you want to continue the series. However, if you're wrapping up things you may not want to open that door, so perhaps you build-in a reason that the sister is only in the story world for a short time like she lives in another city or country.

- *Explain Changes*

If you do need to make a change to something that's already in the story world, then be sure to describe what's happened. If your protagonist lived in a basement apartment in Book One, then lives in the penthouse in Book Two, you have to explain the change.

DETAILS, DETAILS: KEEPING TRACK

Since the little details are so important, keeping track of them is critical. But how to do it? I'm sure there are as many ways to do this as there are writers, but here are a few techniques you can use to track all the minutia. You'll have to experiment and find the system that works best for with your personality and writing style.

- ### *Series Bible*

Some authors create a separate document to record the details of their books and series. Some authors use a spreadsheet, while others use a Word doc. There are also software options like StoryShop, which is specifically designed for writers. But you can use any organizing or project management app to track your story world.

I recently began creating lists of characters, places, and plot ideas in Trello. I like the ability to add images to my notes. It works for me because it's visual and not too overwhelming.

- ### *Outsource Series Bible Creation*

But what if you're already deep into your series or literary universe and you didn't document the details? Don't worry, you still have options. Some virtual assistants offer the service of creating a story bible for you. Or you can ask a reader to do it for you. Have them re-read the series, noting down important details.

Whether it's an assistant or a super fan, you'll want certain aspects of the story recorded. At a minimum, you'll want to know names, physical descriptions of characters, relationships between characters, significant details about locations, and any special issues related to your world, such as magic systems, government, and language.

• *Searching and Re-reading*

What if you're in the middle of a book and don't have the time to wait for a series bible to be completed? The search option is your friend! I didn't have a series bible for my first series. I wrote it in Word and Control/Command + F was my go-to maneuver when I needed to find a detail that was fuzzy.

If you're not limited on time, another option is to re-read earlier books. Some authors re-read every book in a series before they begin a new book in the series to make sure all the details are fresh in their memory. As your series gets longer and your literary universe bigger, re-reading everything may not make sense, time-wise. You might be better off paying someone to create a series bible at that point.

- *Batch-writing*

Batch-writing is another way to keep your mind "in the series" so that the details aren't so difficult to recall.

DEALING WITH A STUCK CHARACTER

If a protagonist doesn't change and grow then the character can feel as if they're looping through the same story with a *Groundhog Day*-like repetition. This situation can cause readers to feel frustrated. You have several options to unstick your character.

- *Launch your character on a new arc or weave a new subplot into the story*

Check out the Character Arcs and Subplot chapter for ideas.

- *Give your character small arcs and challenges*

Even if you're writing a flat arc protagonist, she can still change in small ways. Perhaps your protagonist learns something about being too trusting in Book One. If you callback to that lesson-learned in a future book with your protagonist being more cautious that shows the reader your character has changed and grown.

You can also give your protagonist small challenges in each book. Maybe they want to open a new location for their business or give a speech without breaking out in a sweat.

The challenges can be simple. In the novella *Menace at the Christmas Market*, Kate is looking for the perfect Christmas gift for her boyfriend, but she's sidetracked by mystery and intrigue. It's only at the end of the novella that she finds the right present. The search for the gift frames the novella and gives Kate (and readers) the experience of the search as well as the satisfaction of a goal achieved.

Other types of challenges you could use include:

- Goals—run a marathon or get out of town for the weekend
- Relationships—mend a broken relationship or break off a toxic one
- Status—a promotion at work or purchase of a car or house
- Return to "normal" or a "new normal"—get back to work after an injury or settle into a new routine after a divorce

- Transitions—handoff a job at work or send a kid off to college

STUCK IN A LOVE TRIANGLE

If your characters are stuck in a romantic subplot that is a love triangle, you've got two options. You can either decide that your character will never decide, or pick one corner of the triangle and end the suspense.

Both choices—keeping your characters in suspended animation, or ending the live triangle—have risks. If your protagonist continues to waffle between the two options, some readers will eventually drop off because they're tired of waiting to see what happens. If your readers are divided in their loyalty, say part of them are on #TeamBadBoy and part are on #TeamBoyNextDoor, and you decide to end the love triangle, then you'll tick off some of your readers.

If you decide to end the love triangle you've got a couple of options. Author Sandra Orchard let her fans vote on her website for who her protagonist would be with in the Serena Jones series.[1] Then Orchard wrote the winning choice into the series.

You could go that route, or you could layer in foreshadowing to prepare readers for the protagonist's decision. You may have fallout from unhappy readers if you end the love triangle, but it could also be the start of a new arc for your protagonist and launch the series in a new direction.

WEAK BOOK ONE

As we write more books, we hone our craft and produce better books, so our first book in the series may be the weakest book. You can do a couple of things to remedy a weak Book One.

- ***Rewrite***

You could rewrite the book. You have to decide if the time investment is worth it. And even if you do rewrite it, you'll still have the reviews show up from the original book, unless you republish it as a new edition.

- ***Rework or relaunch***

A suggestion in Episode 216 of the SPA Girls podcast is to either rework your first book or write a new series. If you rework your series, can you rework Book Two and make it Book One? Could your Book One become bonus material, or a side-story, or prequel? If the story doesn't lend itself to reworking, you may decide to cut your losses and move on to write a new series.

MINDSET ISSUE

BOREDOM

Boredom is probably the number one problem authors face when it comes to writing a series. The siren song of the shiny new idea is strong. If you're bored with writing a series, your discontent may come through in the writing.

If you want to continue writing a series after the initial spark is gone, you have to find a way to make it interesting. With the caveat that you always want to stay within genre expectations, here are some ways to keep a series fresh:

- *New character(s)*

Introducing a new character (or characters) to the mix can reinvigorate a series. I found this to work well when the new character was an antagonist.

When a rival professional organizer arrives in the small town where military spouse Ellie is the only part-time professional organizer, Ellie suddenly has business competition, which added a new dimension to the series. I added in the extra layer that the two women had to work together to solve the mystery, and

I had a fresh concept that I found interesting to write about.

The caution with introducing a new character is that the character should add some extra element or twist to the story. We're all familiar with sitcoms that added a new cute kid to the cast when the original kids grew up and the only role for the new kid was to take the place of the old kids. Avoid recycling characters.

• *Explore a secondary character's backstory*

Is there a secondary character you could get to know better? The background of a curmudgeonly character in my Murder on Location series provided a subplot for *Death in an Elegant City* when I began to think about why he was always so irritated and annoyed.

• *Delve into a theme*

Sometimes a theme can give you a creative burst. For instance, have you written a book with a holiday theme? Halloween, Christmas, and Valentine's Day are all popular themes you could explore. Or is there a certain type of trope that's popular in your genre that you haven't written about yet?

- ***Put a new twist on a classic trope***

Agatha Christie is famous for the clever twists she put on mystery genre as she pushed the boundaries. She experimented with the element of who the murderer was, toggling through options: the sidekick, the investigating officer, and even all the suspects.

In *The Body in the Library*, she plays with a well-known trope from classic detective fiction. In the Forward she describes how she wanted to create a novel that was variation on the classic trope with a traditional library, but the murder victim would be the sort of a person who would very likely never be found in that location.

We've already covered how Agatha Christie wanted to write about other characters besides Poirot, but wasn't able to because of the dictates from her publisher. I wonder if the limit of having to write about certain characters pushed her inventiveness into plot and structure.

Embrace the limits of your genre and structure, but see if you can push against them to create something new. How can you twist a trope to surprise and delight readers?

- ***Try a new style or structure***

Sometimes changing the style or structure of a story can reinvigorate you. Try writing in a different tense or change up the structure.

If you always have a single POV, add another POV or two. If you always have a dead body in chapter three, move it to chapter one. You can change up any structure element: tense, POV, pacing, setting, etc.

QUESTIONS

How can you handle a large cast of secondary characters?

What issues will you face regarding immutability in your genre?

_____

_____

_____

_____

_____

_____

What problems do you foresee with series characters?

_____

_____

_____

_____

_____

_____

How will you keep track of the details?

_____

_____

_____

_____

_____

_____

_____

What arc, subplot, or challenge could you give a stuck character?

_____

_____

_____

_____

_____

_____

_____

Will you use a love triangle as a subplot in your series? Will it be a perpetual love triangle or will you resolve the romantic subplot?

If you have a weak Book One, which option is your best choice: rewrite it or rework the series order? Why?

How will you keep boredom at bay? Which tactic is the best for you as a writer and blends well with your genre?

_____

_____

_____

_____

_____

_____

_____

NOTES

_____

_____

_____

_____

_____

_____

_____

_____

_____

_____

_____

_____

MARKETING

*"Buying a book is not about obtaining a possession,
but about securing a portal."*
—*Laura Miller*

A series is more than a group of linked books that draw the reader through the novels. That connectedness has built-in evergreen marketing potential.

You'll focus most of your marketing materials and budget on the first book in the series. Book One is like an engine, funneling interested readers on to the rest of the books. You keep topping up the funnel with potential readers, and some of them will filter through to subsequent books.

This type of focused marketing plan has the advantage of simplicity. It's easier to promote a single Book One instead of several different stand-alone books.

There are many evergreen marketing tactics you can use with a series, including perma-free, price pulsing and discounting. We'll focus on ebooks, but the tactics can work for other formats as well.

BOOK ONE AS A PERMA-FREE

All the ebook retailers except Amazon allow you to price your ebook at zero. Once you do that, Amazon will price-match (in most cases) and you'll have a permanently free ebook, a perma-free. With no payment barrier, a perma-free makes it easy for readers to give your book a try.

Drawbacks

The downside of perma-free is that readers may not value a book they downloaded at no cost. It may sit on their e-reader for months, or years, unopened. Another drawback is you may get downloads from readers who aren't aligned with your genre. They may really want a sweet romance book, but they download your steamy romance because it has their favorite friends-to-lovers trope. If they read it and aren't happy, they may review it unfavorably.

Despite the drawbacks, a perma-free book is still a valuable promotion tool you can use to attract readers. Most people love a bargain, and getting something for free is a big lure.

Benefits

• *Open promotion option*

With a perma-free book you always have something you can use to promote your series without the hassle of price changes. You can even set up a rolling promotion schedule with a prema-free, rotating through the different discount sites, hitting various readers throughout the year. Or you can run constant low-budget ads to your perma-free to continue to bring people into your series.

• *Mailing List Magnet*

You can also use a perma-free as a reader magnet to encourage mailing list signups. You might think that because the book is free on all vendors, you won't get many signups, but I didn't find that to be the case. I used my perma-free as a reader magnet for at least a year and saw a steady influx of new readers.

• *Filter Advance Reading Team*

I also use the perma-free to filter my advance reading team. I have no qualms about asking readers who sign up for my team to link to at least one review to show they're readers who post reviews.

I get requests from people who'd like to join my team who say, "I've never read your books, but I'd like to." If they can't download a perma-free and post a review, they don't get a place on my Reading Team.

PRICE PULSING TO FREE

If you don't want to lower the price of your book to zero permanently, you could price pulse. You drop your price to free for a short period, then return your book to regular price. This tactic has the advantage of making your book attractive to bargain-hunters, then you can return it to full-price and capture more sales at the higher price since the drop to free has raised the visibility of your book.

The disadvantage to price pulsing is that you may still get freebie-seekers who grab the book, but don't read it—or you have readers who aren't aligned with your genre, but download it anyway, which can result in negative reviews. However, since you're only dropping your price for a short period of time, you may be able to limit negative reviews.

PRICE DROPS

Another tactic to drive sales to your series is to drop the price, but not all the way to free. The likelihood of a reader opening your book increases when a reader pays something for it—even if it's only ninety-nine cents or two dollars. They want to get their money's worth, even if it's a couple of bucks!

A nice aspect of using price drops is you can attract readers at different price points. **Freebie-seekers** will only give a new author a try if the book is free. **Bargain shoppers** look for books discounted to around two dollars and below. **Less price-sensitive readers** will buy books at higher prices. A steeper discount can make your sale more compelling. If you're discounting a higher price, say $5.99 to $1.99, that big markdown may be more attractive to some shoppers than a $2.99 book discounted to ninety-nine cents.

PRICE DROPS ON LATER BOOKS IN THE SERIES

While you generally will concentrate your price drops on Book One, you can also discount later books in the series. Some authors cycle through their series, regularly dropping the price on each book to draw in new readers.

This system can work well. Readers may go back to the beginning of the series and read through to the book they bought on sale, then continue on to the end.

I've used this technique a few times, discounting Book Two, but I've been hesitant to rotate through each book in a series. I didn't want to set the expectation with my readers that if they wait, the later books will eventually go on sale.

However, other authors have found rotating discounts are an effective way to increase their readership. I think the size of your backlist impacts this decision. If you have a large catalog, cycling price drops could be an effective tactic.

STAIR-STEP PRICING

Another marketing tactic you can use with a series is stair-step pricing. You price the first book at a low price point, which could be anywhere from perma-free up to a few dollars, then the subsequent books in the series are priced higher.

The pattern might look like perma-free for Book One, $2.99 for Book Two, then $4.99 for Book Three and beyond. Or you can set a lower price for Book One, then all other books in the series are priced the same, say $4.99 or $5.99.

PREQUELS, BONUS EPILOGUES, SHORT STORIES, AND CROSSOVERS

Related content is a fantastic way to market your series. Your readers love your literary universe, and they want more of it. Give it to them with prequels, bonus epilogues, and short stories. As Damon Coutnery, founder of Bookfunnel said, "Your readers will never be upset with you for giving them more content."

Most of these types of extra content (except the bonus epilogue) can do double-duty. You can give your newsletter readers a short story as bonus material, then later you can put the content up for sale or repurpose it in another way. It's recycling and up-cycling of your content.

Prequels

A prequel makes a great reader magnet. Book One of the High Society series mentions Lady Sophia's sapphires and how Olive sorted out the problem and helped the family to avoid an embarrassing situation.

I intentionally included the mention of the jewels, but didn't describe what happened. I wrote a short story, *Lady Sophia's Sapphires*, which I sent to my newsletter list as a Christmas gift, then I modified the back matter in *Murder at Archly Manor*, the first book in the High Society Lady Detective series. Anyone who signs up for my newsletter gets the bonus story of Olive's first "case."

. . .

Bonus Epilogue

A bonus epilogue (a continuation of the story, not the actual conclusion of the book) is a huge incentive to sign up for your mailing list. These are especially popular in romance. The couple has a Happily Ever After at the end of the book, then the bonus epilogue shows them at their wedding or when they have a baby.

Short Stories

Short stories can throw the spotlight on secondary characters, fill gaps in the narrative, or give more explanation and background to the main story. They can be used as bonus material and reader magnets.

You can submit them to literary publications and anthologies, which can widen your audience. You can also add them to bundles, giving the bundle new content and making it tempting to both new and established readers. And you can put several of them together and create a short story collection. M.L. Buchman sells his short stories in ebook and print and also records them in audio himself, then puts the audio up for sale.

Crossover Books

A crossover book brings two protagonists from

different series together in a single book, which can boost sales of both series. I'm using this tactic with *Duplicity*, as I mentioned in the chapter about spinoffs and literary universes. You could also use a crossover book in your autoresponder series to introduce new readers to several of your series.

BUNDLES

Another way to market your series is through bundles, which are sometimes called box sets. Collecting several of your books together and pricing them at a discount can pull new readers into your series. Bundles are usually priced at a discount, compared to purchasing the books individually, which makes the bundle attractive to cost-conscious readers.

- ***Take Advantage of the Binge-watching Trend***

A trend in entertainment is binge-watching. Streaming services allow people to consume movie trilogies and whole seasons of episodic shows. Bundles appeal to this desire to get everything at once. All the books packaged together in one convenient set makes it ideal for readers who want to binge-read or binge-listen.

• *Bundling Options*

Bundles are usually put together in sets of three: Books 1-3, 4-6, and so on. Another tactic that appeals to binge-readers and binge-listeners is to bundle the whole series together.

Currently, it's only cost-effective to do this on non-Amazon retailers because Amazon caps the seventy percent royalty at $9.99, but putting together a bundle of several books or the whole series is a great way to get traction on the non-Amazon retailers. If you have several series you can also create a sampler bundle that contains the first book from each series.

• *Bonus Content to Draw New Readers*

You can add bonus content such as a new short story or novella to your bundle to draw in established readers as well as new readers. New readers will be getting a deal because of the new material that's included.

If you don't like the idea of established readers having to pay for a bundle to get the new content, you can give the new material to your newsletter subscribers first before it goes into the bundle.

• *Strategic Releases*

Release your bundles strategically to maximize your profit. Publish individual books first, then after the books have been out for a while, perhaps several months or a year, bundle the first three. Continue the pattern of releasing individual books, then bundling them after a certain period of time.

QUESTIONS

Which pricing tactic will you use for your series?

_____

_____

_____

_____

_____

_____

What series marketing strategies will you use?

_____

_____

_____

_____

_____

_____

_____

Jot down any ideas for extra material you could write that would give you marketing content for prequels, bonus epilogues, short stories, and crossovers.

_____

_____

_____

_____

_____

_____

_____

How could you creatively bundle your series content?

_____

_____

_____

_____

_____

_____

_____

NOTES

SERIOUS SERIES OVERWHELM

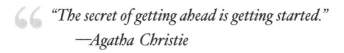 *"The secret of getting ahead is getting started."*
  —Agatha Christie

I realize that all these details and options for constructing and marketing a series may actually paralyze some writers. My intention was to spark ideas—not stop you in your tracks.

If you're overwhelmed with options and techniques, then focus on Book One. Follow the advice of my all-time favorite writing quote from Maxwell Perkins, "Just get it down on paper. Then we'll see what to do about it."

Finish the first book in your series, then step back

and assess it. Sometimes it's easier to work with actual text than abstract ideas. Don't get bogged down in planning.

If you never actually write Book One, you'll never have a series. All the plans in the world are wonderful, but you need to get the words down and produce books to actually have a series. So write those books! And connect them into a series!

NOTES

_____

_____

_____

_____

_____

_____

_____

_____

_____

_____

_____

_____

_____

NOTES

WHY WRITE A SERIES?

1. http://archive.ph/VioyE
2. http://www.bbc.com/culture/story/20160106-how-sherlock-holmes-changed-the-world

PROTAGONIST WITH A FLAT CHARACTER ARC

1. https://www.helpingwritersbecomeauthors.com/flat-character-arc-1/

SERIES PATTERNS

1. http://www.screenwritingtricks.com/2011/05/rule-of-three.html

CLIFFHANGERS AND READ-THROUGH HOOKS

1. https://www.etymonline.com/word/cliff-hanger#etymonline_v_28188

TROUBLESHOOTING

1. http://sandraorchard.com/vote-for-your-favorite/

APPENDIX 1

RESOURCES

- Alexandra Sokoloff post —"Rule of Three"
- BBC Article about Agatha Christie's attitude toward Poirot—"How Agatha Christie grew to dislike Hercule Poirot"
- BBC Article about the reaction to the death of Sherlock Holmes—"How Sherlock Holmes Changed the World"
- K.M. Weiland post on HelpingWritersBecomeAuthors.com—"How to Write a Flat Character Arc—Part I"
- M.L. Bachman
- Novel Marketing Podcast

- Online Etymology Dictionary—definition of *cliffhanger*
- Sandra Orchard poll on SandraOrchard.com —"Vote For Your Favorite"
- *Save the Cat* by Blake Snyder
- *Screenwriting Tricks for Authors* by Alexandra Sokoloff
- SPA Girls Podcast

APPENDIX 2

QUESTION ARCHIVE

You can also find a downloadable list of questions at SaraRosett.com/SeriesQuestions.

Introduction

- Make a list of your favorite series books. Do you see any similarities?
- Do they have the same type of protagonist? Are there any common themes or subplots?
- If you've written a series before, list what was successful about it.
- Also take a moment to list the problems you encountered.

Types of Series
If You're Planning A Multi-Protagonist Series

- How will you link the series?
- Will you have an antagonist?
- How will the secondary characters take center stage in the following books?
- What is the setting? How will it appeal to fans of your genre? What sort of world-building do you need to do?
- What subplots will you have?
- How many books will be in your series initially?

If You're Planning A Single Protagonist Series With A Flat Arc

- How will you make the main character interesting? How will you make sure the protagonist doesn't seem to be boring compared to the secondary characters and the antagonist?
- How will the secondary characters change around the protagonist?
- Will you have a single antagonist through the series or different ones in each book?
- What is the setting? How will it appeal to

fans of your genre? How will the setting
impact the series? Is it too limited?

- What world-building do you need to do?
- What subplots will you have? Will they flow
  throughout the series or be episodic?
- Does your series have an end-point or is it
  open-ended?

If You're Planning A Single Protagonist Series With A Robust Arc

- How does the protagonist change in each
  book as well as over the course of the series?
- Will any secondary characters have a
  strong arc?
- Are any secondary characters foils/mirrors of
  the protagonist?
- Will you have a single antagonist through the
  series or different ones in each book?
- What is the setting? How will it appeal to fans
  of your genre? How will the setting impact the
  series? What world-building do you need to do?
- What subplots will you have? Will they flow
  throughout the series or be confined to each
  book?
- What is the end point of your protagonist's
  arc? Will that be the end of the series? How

could you extend the series, if you'd like to continue writing it after the initial arc is complete?

If You're Not Sure Which Type Of Series You Should Use

- Which is most common for your genre, multi-protagonist or single protagonist series? List examples of popular series in your genre as a jumping-off point for brainstorming your series.
- Which type of series appeals to you most, one with multiple protagonists or one with a single protagonist? Why?
- If you're considering a single protagonist series, which type of arc would be best for your character, flat or robust?
- Once you've decided on a series type, what are the drawbacks or challenges you might need to deal with?

Character Arcs and Subplots

- What character arcs appeal to you from the ones listed in this section?
- Can you think of other arcs?
- Which arcs will you use in your series?

- What subplots appeal to you from the ones listed in this section?
- Can you think of other subplots?
- What subplots do you often see in your genre?
- Which subplots will you use in your series?

Series Patterns

- Which series pattern will you use? Why?
- What subplots will you use to pull readers through the series?
- If you need to cut the series short, can you end it early? How will you wrap up the subplots and open threads in a satisfying way for the reader at an earlier point than you originally planned?

Cliffhangers and Read-Through Hooks

- List the books that you waited anxiously for the next book in the series. What sort of endings did the author use?
- What sort of endings will the individual books in your series have? Will you use a cliffhanger? Why or why not?
- What kind of read-through hook could you use at the end of each book to give your

reader a taste of the next one?

Batch Writing

- If you're interested in batch-writing, do you have time in your production schedule to write several books back-to-back?
- If you need to make adjustments to your schedule, how will you do that?
- Can you afford to bank the books and hold them until you have several finished?

Ending a Series

- List the book series that you've lost interest in. Why did you stop reading them?
- List the book series that ended in a satisfying way. What did you like about the endings? Why were they satisfying?
- What issues around ending a series do you struggle with? Are they mechanical or mindset issues? If they're mechanical, make a list of topics to research to help you with the craft aspects. If they're mindset, how will you transition your thinking?
- If you have to end a series, which approach to telling your readers appeals to you? Why?

Connecting a Series: Spinoffs and Literary Universes

- List your favorite spinoff characters. What do you love about them?
- List the spinoff characters that didn't work for you. Why didn't they appeal to you?
- What characters could you spinoff from your series?
- What literary universes do you enjoy? What is it about them that appeals to you?
- How could you expand your series into a literary universe?
- What companion books could you create to further expand Your literary universe?
- If your series is a retelling, what unique spin will you put on the original material? Will your take appeal to readers of the original?

Extending a Series

- How could you extend your original storyline?
- What new subplot could you add to your original story to give it new life?
- Do any aspects of your genre tropes or conventions give you ideas for reviving the series?

- What could you do to give your characters a reset?

Troubleshooting

- How can you handle a large cast of secondary characters?
- What issues will you face regarding immutability in your genre?
- What problems do you foresee with series characters?
- How will you keep track of the details?
- What arc, subplot, or challenge could you give a stuck character?
- Will you use a love triangle as a subplot in your series? Will it be a perpetual love triangle or will you resolve the romantic subplot?
- If you have a weak Book One, which option is your best choice: rewrite it or rework the series order? Why?
- How will you keep boredom at bay? Which tactic is the best for you as a writer and blends well with your genre?

Marketing

- Which pricing tactic will you use for your series?

- What series marketing strategies will you use?
- Jot down any ideas for extra material you could write that would give you marketing content for prequels, bonus epilogues, short stories, or crossovers.
- How could you creatively bundle your series content?

ALSO BY SARA ROSETT

This is Sara's complete catalogue at the time of publication, but new books are in the works. To be the first to find out when Sara has a new book, sign up for her updates.

Murder on Location series

Death in the English Countryside

Death in an English Cottage

Death in a Stately Home

Death in an Elegant City

Menace at the Christmas Market (novella)

Death in an English Garden

Death at an English Wedding

High Society Lady Detective series

Murder at Archly Manor

Murder at Blackburn Hall

The Egyptian Antiquities Murder

Murder in Black Tie

Old Money Murder in Mayfair

ABOUT THE AUTHOR

USA Today bestselling author Sara Rosett writes fun mysteries. Her books are light-hearted escapes for readers who enjoy interesting settings, atmospheric settings, and puzzling mysteries. *Publishers Weekly* called Sara's books, "satisfying," "well-executed," and "sparkling."

Sara loves to get new stamps in her passport and considers dark chocolate a daily requirement. Find out more at SaraRosett.com.

Connect with Sara
www.SaraRosett.com

Made in the USA
Coppell, TX
11 February 2021